Your Government:
How It Works

The History of the Republican Party

Norma Jean Lutz

Arthur M. Schlesinger, jr.
Senior Consulting Editor

Chelsea House Publishers
Philadelphia

CHELSEA HOUSE PUBLISHERS
Editor in Chief Stephen Reginald
Production Manager Pamela Loos
Art Director Sara Davis
Director of Photography Judy L. Hasday
Managing Editor James D. Gallagher
Senior Production Editor LeeAnne Gelletly

Staff for THE HISTORY OF THE REPUBLICAN PARTY
Project Editor Anne Hill
Project Editor/Publishing Coordinator Jim McAvoy
Associate Art Director Takeshi Takahashi
Series Designer Takeshi Takahashi, Keith Trego

The Chelsea House World Wide Web address is
http://www.chelseahouse.com

First Printing
1 3 5 7 9 8 6 4 2

Library of Congress Cataloging-in-Publication Data

Lutz, Norma Jean.
      The history of the Republican Party / by Norma Jean Lutz.
            p. cm. — (Your government—how it works)
      Includes bibliographical references and index.
      Summary: Traces the origins of the Republican Party, discussing
key figures, conventions, platforms, and its organization.
      ISBN 0-7910-5540-X (hc)
      1. Republican Party (U.S. : 1854-)—History—Juvenile litera-
ture. [1. Republican Party (U.S. : 1854-)—History. 2. Political
parties. 3. United States—Politics and governent.] I. Title.
II. Series.

JK2356 .L92 2000
342.2734'09—dc21   99-048458

Contents

Introduction

Government: Crises of Confidence

Arthur M. Schlesinger, jr.

FROM THE START, Americans have regarded their government with a mixture of reliance and mistrust. The men who founded the republic understood the importance of government. "If men were angels," observed the 51st Federalist Paper, "no government would be necessary." But men are not angels. Because human beings are subject to wicked as well as to noble impulses, government was deemed essential to assure freedom and order.

The American revolutionaries, however, also knew that government could become a source of injury and oppression. The men who gathered in Philadelphia in 1787 to write the Constitution therefore had two purposes in mind: They wanted to establish a strong central authority and to limit that central authority's capacity to abuse its power.

To prevent the abuse of power, the Founding Fathers wrote two basic principles into the Constitution. The principle of federalism divided power between the state governments and the central authority. The principle of the separation of powers subdivided the central authority itself into three branches—the executive, the legislative, and the judiciary—so that "each may be a check on the other."

YOUR GOVERNMENT: HOW IT WORKS examines some of the major parts of that central authority, the federal government. It explains how various officials, agencies, and departments operate and explores the political organizations that have grown up to serve the needs of government.

Introduction

The federal government as presented in the Constitution was more an idealistic construct than a practical administrative structure. It was barely functional when it came into being.

This was especially true of the executive branch. The Constitution did not describe the executive branch in any detail. After vesting executive power in the president, it assumed the existence of "executive departments" without specifying what these departments should be. Congress began defining their functions in 1789 by creating the Departments of State, Treasury, and War.

President Washington, assisted by Secretary of the Treasury Alexander Hamilton, equipped the infant republic with a working administrative structure. Congress also continued that process by creating more executive departments as they were needed.

Throughout the 19th century, the number of federal government workers increased at a consistently faster rate than did the population. Increasing concerns about the politicization of public service led to efforts—bitterly opposed by politicians—to reform it in the latter part of the century.

The 20th century saw considerable expansion of the federal establishment. More importantly, it saw growing impatience with bureaucracy in society as a whole.

The Great Depression during the 1930s confronted the nation with its greatest crisis since the Civil War. Under Franklin Roosevelt, the New Deal reshaped the federal government, assigning it a variety of new responsibilities and greatly expanding its regulatory functions. By 1940, the number of federal workers passed the 1 million mark.

Critics complained of big government and bureaucracy. Business owners resented federal regulation. Conservatives worried about the impact of paternalistic government on self-reliance, on community responsibility, and on economic and personal freedom.

When the United States entered World War II in 1941, government agencies focused their energies on supporting the war effort. By the end of World War II, federal civilian employment had risen to 3.8 million. With peace, the federal establishment declined to around 2 million in 1950. Then growth resumed, reaching 2.8 million by the 1980s.

A large part of this growth was the result of the national government assuming new functions such as: affirmative action in civil rights, environmental protection, and safety and health in the workplace.

Some critics became convinced that the national government was a steadily growing behemoth swallowing up the liberties of the people. The 1980s brought new intensity to the debate about government growth. Foes of Washington bureaucrats preferred local government, feeling it more responsive to popular needs.

But local government is characteristically the government of the locally powerful. Historically, the locally powerless have often won their human and constitutional rights by appealing to the national government. The national government has defended racial justice against local bigotry, upheld the Bill of Rights against local vigilantism, and protected natural resources from local greed. It has civilized industry and secured the rights of labor organizations. Had the states' rights creed prevailed, perhaps slavery would still exist in the United States.

Americans are still of two minds. When pollsters ask large, spacious questions—Do you think government has become too involved in your lives? Do you think government should stop regulating business?—a sizable majority opposes big government. But when asked specific questions about the practical work of government—Do you favor Social Security? Unemployment compensation? Medicare? Health and safety standards in factories? Environmental protection?— a sizable majority approves of intervention.

We do not like bureaucracy, but we cannot live without it. We need its genius for organizing the intricate details of our daily lives. Without bureaucracy, modern society would collapse. It would be impossible to run any of the large public and private organizations we depend on without bureaucracy's division of labor and hierarchy of authority. The challenge is to keep these necessary structures of our civilization flexible, efficient, and capable of innovation.

More than 200 years after the drafting of the Constitution, Americans still rely on government but also mistrust it. These attitudes continue to serve us well. What we mistrust, we are more likely to monitor. And government needs our constant attention if it is to avoid inefficiency, incompetence, and arbitrariness. Without our informed participation, it cannot serve us individually or help us as a people to attain the lofty goals of the Founding Fathers.

Abraham Lincoln, the first Republican president of the United States, achieved the primary goal he had on taking office: to save the Union. In this symbolic image, the American flag represents the preserved Union; the eagle and fasces (bundle of rods with projecting ax blades) on Lincoln's chair symbolize the republic; and the Emancipation Proclamation held in his left hand stands for the abolition of slavery.

CHAPTER 1

Born in Revolt (1854)

ON MAY 16, 1860, newspaper reporters sat atop the roof of a two-story meeting hall near the Chicago River in Chicago, Illinois. The building was nicknamed "The Wigwam." At the Wigwam's grand entryway arched a wooden crescent, bearing the name Republican Party Headquarters. Square turrets at each corner of the roof were topped with flagpoles flying Old Glory. Ten thousand party members filled the seats inside and packed the upper gallery, which stretched across three sides of the rectangular wooden building. Ten thousand more stood outside in the dirt streets, unable to get in, all wanting to be the first to learn the news. Who would be the Republican **candidate** for president of the United States? Reporters on the roof were ready to shout the news to the multitude below. The brass cannon out front stood ready to fire; the telegraph lines would flash the news to the entire nation.

The noisy, boisterous crowds were well aware that history was in the making. The convention hall, decked out in red, white, and blue garlands, ribbons, streamers, banners, flags, and bunting reflected the excitement.

This momentous occasion had been many years in the making. In the previous decade many small political groups had split off from the two major parties—the Democrats and the Whigs.

Split-offs had often taken place before, but never had a new political group been so large, so united, or so powerful. The Republican party was definitely making its voice heard.

Deepening Differences

Usually a new political group forms because citizens are in revolt, or in opposition, to something. This situation was especially true with the Republicans. Those who came to make up the new party were in violent opposition to the institution of slavery. They felt the slave owners of the South, referred to as the slavocracy, were ruling Congress and running the entire nation.

Although the main disagreement between the North and the South was the issue of slavery, other differences existed as well. Manufacturing was mainly concentrated in New England and the Middle Atlantic states. Most of the wealth, therefore, was in the North.

This 18th-century painting shows slaves in Sunday dress dancing and making music outside their quarters. Disagreement over slavery strongly divided the North and the South.

Interior of a typical 18th-century machine shop. Although most industry and wealth were concentrated in the North, many Southerners wanted to hold onto their agricultural-based way of life.

Fast-running rivers, needed to generate power for factories, were missing in the South. Even if they had had the needed water power, most Southerners would not have liked the industrialized way of living found in the North. They saw no reason to exchange their rural plantation lifestyle for factories and industry.

Soil differed as well. The soil in the North was less fertile compared to the rich soil of the South. The South also had warmer weather and longer growing seasons.

Many Northerners—especially shippers in New York City—conducted a great deal of business with Southerners. Packet lines brought cotton to New York and reloaded it to be shipped across the Atlantic to England. The cotton trade brought wealth to many New Englanders. In spite of this fact, grassroots protest in the North swelled against slavery. Meanwhile in the political world, Congress attempted to create **compromise** after compromise to appease both the North and the South.

Compromises

As new states were added to the Union, an attempt was made to keep the number of slave states equal to the number of free states. Each new state meant representation in Congress, and neither side wanted the other to have more

Land gained by the United States in its war with Mexico (California, New Mexico, and Texas) is shown in pink on this territorial map.

power. One attempt at equalization resulted in the Missouri Compromise of 1820.

In this compromise, Missouri was admitted as a slave state and at the same time Maine was admitted as a free state. In addition, the compromise established a line westward, above which slavery was not allowed except in the state of Missouri. This 36°30' line (36 degrees 30 minutes north latitude, marking the area on a map where slavery was or wasn't accepted) was designed to settle the dispute for at least 30 years.

In 1846 the United States' war with Mexico resulted in two new territories (California and New Mexico) for the United States and nearly doubled the size of Texas. The question again arose: should these states be slave or free?

David Wilmot, a Pennsylvania Democrat, proposed an amendment that prohibited slavery in any territory acquired from Mexico. The Wilmot **Proviso,** as it was called, was twice defeated in the Senate. The South declared that Congress had no power to prohibit slavery.

Senator Stephen A. Douglas from Illinois suggested a solution, which he called popular **sovereignty.** This proposal suggested that settlers in each state or territory vote to decide whether they wanted slavery or not. The problem was that the popular sovereignty proposal did not say when the settlers should vote nor how long the decisions should stand.

Yet Another Compromise

On January 29, 1850, yet another compromise was introduced in the Senate, which served to strengthen the Fugitive Slave Act. Senator William H. Seward of New York, a Conscience Whig, strongly argued against the compromise. He stated that there was "a higher law than the Constitution."

President Zachary Taylor was also against the bill, but he died in office and was succeeded by Vice President Millard Fillmore who was not as firmly opposed to it. In the end the Compromise of 1850 passed by bits and pieces with the help of Senator Douglas.

The Final Blow

Four years later Senator Douglas introduced the Kansas-Nebraska Bill in January of 1854. Making arrangements with the Southern politicians, Douglas divided the large Nebraska Territory into two states, Kansas and Nebraska. Nothing was said as to whether they would be slave or free. Douglas said he would leave that to the settlers by popular vote. The bill set off a furor throughout the North.

When the Kansas-Nebraska Bill became law, the Missouri Compromise of 1820 was broken because Kansas was north of the 36°30' line. Douglas was totally unprepared for the anger that resulted. The bill shredded the last strip of peace between North and South. It broke apart not only regions but political parties as well. As an outcome of this law, Northern Whigs vehemently disagreed with

Southern Whigs; Northern Democrats were at odds with Southern Democrats.

In Kansas the settlers were to decide the slavery issue. However, organized proslavery Missourians, called "border ruffians," came into Kansas and voted illegally. The conflict erupted into a small civil war, causing the state to be known as "bleeding Kansas."

The final blow before the Civil War was a decision handed down by the Supreme Court in the Dred Scott case. The Court, dominated by Democrats, ruled that a slave had no civil rights and therefore could not sue in federal court. The law stated that slaves were property and that Congress could not deprive a person (meaning a white person) of his property without due process of law.

In effect this ruling opened all territories to slavery. The *Chicago Daily Tribune* stated that because of the ruling, Illinois had ceased to be a free state. Now nothing could prevent "opening a slave pen and auction block for the sale of black men, women, and children right here in Chicago."

Birth of the Republican Party

The Republican party, many said, was "leaderless" because it began with hundreds of small gatherings in communities throughout the North to protest the Kansas-Nebraska Act. A few months before the Kansas-Nebraska Bill became law, Whigs, Democrats, and Free-Soilers, met in Ripon, Wisconsin. They agreed that if the bill passed they would work to organize a brand-new party.

Yet another group met a few months later in Michigan, with the same purpose in mind. All across the North, small groups of anti-Nebraskans (meaning they were against the Kansas-Nebraska Bill) came together to put down the forces of slavery. By the spring of 1854, there were anti-Nebraska congressmen who were ready to join the new party.

On July 6, 1854, a mass meeting of 10,000 convened in Jackson, Michigan. The crowd was so large, leaders were forced to move the meeting outside to an oak grove. The group **nominated** candidates for state offices and wrote up a complete platform containing what would become the party's foundation planks. Some historians cite this gathering as the founding of the Republican party.

The new party marked a coming together of many different types of political groups. It affected factory workers in New England as well as homesteaders out West.

Horace Greeley, the well-known editor of the *New York Tribune,* was an avid **abolitionist.** Through his newspaper—read by millions—Greeley voiced his strong support of the new party. He wrote:

> We should not much care whether those . . . thus united were designated Whigs, Free Democrats, or something else; though we think some simple name like Republican would more fitly designate those who have united to restore the Union to its true mission.

In Illinois, one local Whig politician, named Abraham Lincoln, voiced doubts about this new abolitionist movement. The **conservative** Lincoln feared the party might be too radical. He held out the hope that the Whig party might make a comeback. Thus he played no part in the founding of the Republican party. It wasn't until May of 1856 that he signed on with the Illinois Republican party for the first time.

First National Convention

The first Republican nominating convention met from June 17 to 20, 1856, at the Musical Fund Hall in Philadelphia. There the Republicans chose the wealthy John C. Fremont, a former California senator, to be their presidential candidate.

During this convention, Abraham Lincoln made his initial national appearance and was nominated as the vice presidential candidate. In the nomination, he was described as a "prince of good fellows." Even though most of the delegates had never heard him, Lincoln came in second for the office of vice president, losing to a Whig from New Jersey, William L. Dayton. Lincoln campaigned heartily for Fremont.

For a new party, the Republicans fared well at the ballot boxes that fall. They took 42 percent of the major party vote. Most of the moneyed Whigs of the old party, however, voted for the Democratic candidate, James Buchanan. Even more disturbing, the Republicans lost the House of Representatives to the Democrats.

The Republican's Foothold

Upon losing the election, the young party might have fallen apart had it not been for two events. The first was the *Dred Scott* decision, handed down just days after President Buchanan's inauguration. This decision worked to enflame the hearts of the Republican party members.

The second event was an incriminating book written by a Southerner. *Present Crisis in the South,* written by Hinton Rowan Helper, described in detail the economic backwardness caused by slavery. Republicans printed 100,000 copies of the book and distributed them across the nation.

These two events were topped by dire problems in the Buchanan administration. A Wall Street panic hit in the summer of 1857, followed by an economic depression. The president chose to do nothing about the depression and to do nothing about the bloody war in Kansas. Stephen Douglas, author of the Kansas-Nebraska Bill, feuded with, then broke off from, President Buchanan.

At this time Lincoln entered into a series of famous debates with Douglas because both were running for the

Abraham Lincoln waves to the crowd gathered to hear his debate with Stephen Douglas (right) in the 1858 Illinois senatorial race. Although Lincoln lost the election, he gained national recognition as a result of the debates.

senate seat in Illinois. In one of his speeches, Lincoln quoted a Bible Scripture: "A house divided against itself cannot stand." Throughout the Civil War this Scripture became his theme for preserving the nation.

The debates, attended by huge crowds, became celebrations, with cannon salutes, special trains, bands, and fireworks. Although Lincoln lost the election to Douglas, he had made a name for himself. Editor Greeley declared that this homespun lawyer had "the decided advantage" over Douglas.

The stage was now set for the Republican party to make its entry into the political arena.

When the Confederacy attacked Fort Sumter in April 1861, four months after he had taken office as president, Abraham Lincoln became the leader of a nation at war with itself.

CHAPTER **2**

Lincoln at the Helm

Many Candidates

ON THE SURFACE, THE nomination of the first Republican president seemed like a surprise event. The truth, however, was that many people behind the scenes worked hard to make it happen. Party leaders knew it was vital that they have a man who would appeal to all voters, not just to those against slavery. In correspondence with a friend, Greeley wrote, "I want to succeed this time. . . . I mean to have as good a candidate as the majority will elect."

When the 1860 convention was called to order in the Wigwam, only 27 states answered the roll call. The Northern states and the border states were in attendance, but only Virginia and Texas from the South were there. Signs of troubles to come were already evidenced by the absence of the Southern states' representatives.

Abraham Lincoln faced monumental opposition for the nomination. The greatest of these was from William H. Seward, the Whig senator and former governor from New York. Seward, an outspoken opponent of slavery, came over to the Republican party in 1855. Not only did he enjoy national popularity, he commanded the support of moneyed Easterners and controlled New York's 35 electoral votes.

Thousands of Seward supporters stepped off the trains, arriving in Chicago for the convention. His bands played the lively tune "O, Isn't He a Darling?" as they marched through the streets.

Former Ohio governor, Salmon Portland Chase, a newly elected U.S. senator and strong abolitionist, was also in the race. In addition Edward Bates, a former Free-Soil Whig congressman from Missouri, and Supreme Court Justice John McLean, who voted against the *Dred Scott* decision, were prominent in the race.

Behind the Scenes

Norman Judd, a powerful Chicago attorney and close friend of Lincoln's, served on the committee responsible for bringing the convention to the "Garden City," as Chicago was known at the time. Judd, along with Lincoln's manager, Judge David Davis, set up headquarters in the new Tremont House hotel. Here in cigar smoke–filled rooms, Lincoln supporters hammered out deals with Whig delegates.

Likewise, members of the Illinois state Republican convention came to Chicago determined to do what it took to make their "favorite son" the presidential candidate. They wheedled and cajoled other delegates in an attempt to get them to switch support to Lincoln. Suggestions were voiced for running Lincoln as the vice presidential candidate, but Lincoln had previously made it clear he was interested in the presidency or nothing.

The first two days of the convention were spent fashioning the **party platform.** The platform called for the end to the spread of slavery, called for higher **tariffs,** opposed changes to rights of citizenship for immigrants, and spoke against the *Dred Scott* decision. The final adoption of the platform was met with "wild excitement" that was "kept up for ten or fifteen minutes."

Dred Scott, the former slave who lost his 1857 appeal to the Supreme Court for his rights as a United States citizen. The 1860 Republican party platform opposed the decision.

The convention delegates convened for the day, expecting to cast their ballots the next day to elect Seward as the presidential nominee. Greeley sent a telegram to New York stating that Seward would be nominated on the first ballot. As the confident Seward supporters went off to bed, Lincoln supporters worked throughout the night, making deals behind the scenes.

Thousands of Lincoln forces were assembled to make a showing in the Wigwam. When the Seward people arrived at the center the next morning, the Wigwam's main floor and balconies were already filled with shouting men. Lincoln organizers had packed the hall with the loudest shouters in the state. Their shouts and cheers all but drowned out the proceedings. Other delegates were amazed that Lincoln was so popular.

Voter Shifts

The first ballot showed Seward in the lead and Lincoln second. The second ballot saw Pennsylvania shifting its 48 votes to Lincoln. Others followed suit. All of a sudden the Westerners saw a glimmer of hope that their backwoods candidate could win against the moneyed forces of the East. On the third ballot the frontier attorney received 364 votes to Seward's 121$\frac{1}{2}$. The chairman rose to call for a unanimous consent.

Abraham Lincoln waited in Springfield, Illinois, to hear whether he had won the Republican party presidential nomination.

Cannons fired, hats were flung in the air, bands played, and Lincoln's supporters shouted. Uniformed groups of young people known as the Wide Awakes, tramped through the streets, carrying torches and singing, "Ain't You Glad You Joined the Republicans?" Almost as an afterthought, Senator Hannibal Hamlin of Maine was chosen as the vice presidential candidate.

Abraham Lincoln was not inside the Wigwam on that warm day in May. He kept vigil back in Springfield, Illinois, waiting in the newsroom of the *Journal*. When the final news arrived by telegraph, the city exploded into parades and gun salutes. Lincoln, however, politely thanked the crowd and went to bed.

Winning Votes

There were those who thought Lincoln's nomination might split the party. Seward surprised them all by campaigning tirelessly for Lincoln, crisscrossing the North by train. President Lincoln later appointed Seward secretary of state.

The remainder of the country fragmented into three political groups. The Democrats split in two, with the Dixie Democrats holding their own convention in Baltimore. Yet another group, the Constitutional Union party, offered up their candidate.

As was the custom of the day, Lincoln never left Springfield during the **campaign** but greeted thousands of voters in his hometown. On November 6, 1860, Lincoln received the majority of the popular as well as of the electoral college votes. The returns clearly revealed that he would have won even if the three other groups had voted as one force. The people had spoken, and the Republican party was now in the White House.

Party Leadership

Lincoln faced monumental challenges as he took office. Seven states seceded from the Union before his inauguration, four more followed later. On April 10, 1861, at Fort Sumter, South Carolina, the first shots were fired officially launching the bloody Civil War. Never before had the nation been so violently ripped apart.

He stood at the helm of a new political party made up of many different **factions.** Although Lincoln was a conservative, many in the party were radicals who considered him slow and ineffective. During the first year of the war, the president formulated a general political party called the National Union party. The party brought together all Northern Democrats and Republicans as a single unit with the single goal of preserving the Union. Preserving the Union, Lincoln felt, expressed the ultimate reason for fighting the entire war.

In a letter to Greeley, Lincoln wrote:

My paramount object in this struggle is to save the Union, and is not either to save or destroy slavery. . . . What I do about slavery, and the colored race, I do because I believe it helps to save the Union.

Jefferson Davis, president of the Confederate States of America.

The now-famous reply touched Greeley and caused him to throw his support and that of his paper strongly behind the president and the Union party.

The Union party was divided among two groups: those who felt the war should come to a negotiated end (in other words, achieve peace at any cost) and the radicals who believed the war should be fought to the finish. Lincoln used the structure of his political party to harness and direct these differences. He invoked party loyalty to encourage state governors to cooperate with war policies.

Jefferson Davis, president of the Confederate states (the South), had no such party group and suffered because of it. Throughout the war Southern states exercised their belief in states' rights and did as they pleased, often to the point of withholding troops and supplies.

Re-election

By the next election, in 1864, the war still raged on. The Unionist party, the **coalition** of Republicans and Democrats who favored the continuation of the war, renominated Lincoln as their candidate. Andrew Johnson, a former Southern Democrat, seemed to be the good choice as vice president. Those who had remained in the Northern Democratic party nominated General George B. McClelland, a man responsible for the loss of some of the early battles of the war.

Republican parties at the state and local level retained their identity and swung into action. Thousands of pieces of Lincoln literature were mailed out to the fighting Union soldiers. Many soldiers were given leave to come home and cast their votes.

General Sherman's army captured Atlanta two months before the November election. This major turning point in the war infused the North with hope, causing them to vote their president back for a second term.

Loss of a Leader

Lincoln's assassination a week after the end of the war, removed not only a president but also a party leader from office. He was the glue that held the Republican party together. His political skill and popularity had led opposing factions to negotiate their differences and to remain on the same track. His absence was a substantial blow to the party structure. Where it would go from this point no one knew.

This scene from the 1939 film Gone With the Wind *shows Confederate casualties due to the fighting in Atlanta. General Sherman's capture of the city gave the North the confidence to elect Lincoln to a second term as president.*

Congress brought impeachment charges against Lincoln's successor, Andrew Johnson, in 1868. Johnson believed the South should resist the military rule Congress had imposed to enforce governments based on civil rights. He was found not guilty of the charges.

CHAPTER 3

Turn from Radicalism (1865–1896)

REPUBLICAN PARTY MEMBERS SAW Andrew Johnson as a wise selection for vice president in 1864. The choice of a Southern Democrat who remained loyal to the North pleased other Democrats in the Union party. No one considered what type of president he might become.

Political Changes

Lincoln, a Northerner, understood the Northern attitudes toward slavery, race, and the South. Johnson, in contrast, had no real feelings for the North and was almost hostile toward blacks. When Johnson first took leadership of the nation, he was in agreement with the Republican radicals. He agreed with them that the large Southern plantations should be sold off to industrious farmers and that federal troops would be necessary in the South to ensure that emancipation of the slaves was carried out. Later, however, he softened these views, thereby angering the radicals.

President Johnson set up a few simple rules for the South. When the states met the conditions, he planned to restore them to the Union. Southerners quickly met the conditions.

Northerners were infuriated that the programs of emancipation would be left in the hands of white Southerners. They feared that the rights of free blacks would be ignored. The radicals did not believe the South was ready to be reinstated, and they therefore refused to seat Southern congressional members. This led to strained relationships between Johnson and Congress. Ultimately, in 1866, when Congress passed laws to protect ex-slaves, Johnson not only vetoed the laws but broke with the Republican party.

The following year Congress put Southerners under military rule until new governments based on civil rights could be established. Johnson encouraged Southerners to resist this military move, going so far as to remove the secretary of war.

Congress was outraged. Subsequently Johnson was impeached by the House of Representatives and tried before the Senate.

Before the trial could be held, Johnson ceased his interference. New governments were established in the South, and their representatives were admitted back into Congress. Thus the fire went out of the Republican radicals' original anger toward the president. He was found not guilty in his impeachment trial and served the rest of his term in relative peace.

End of Republican Radicals

Johnson's acquittal spelled the end of the radicals in office who had pushed so hard to protect the rights of blacks in the South. The same party who dispatched thousands of troops to Richmond also felt it could dispatch troops to keep the South in line. Although the Republican radicals' motives may have been good, their methods left much to be desired.

Ulysses S. Grant was nominated by the Republican party in 1868 as the man who had won the war.

Johnson moved to the other extreme, leading Southerners to believe they had a right to restoration with no further obligations. The result was bitterness between the races and between geographical sections that remain to this day.

Stalwarts of Grant

The Republicans returned to Chicago for the convention of 1868. They met in the opulent new Crosby Opera House, with its 65 private box seats and seating capacity for 3,000. In gala ceremonies Union military leaders were hailed as conquering heroes.

The military appreciation followed through in the selection of the presidential nominee. Only one name came forth—the general who, in the minds of all, had won the war, Ulysses S. ("Unconditional Surrender") Grant.

The general, meanwhile, was busy working back in Washington, D.C. He later admitted that he was a reluctant candidate. The general, though a genius on the battlefield, knew little about politics. As a result of his lack of political knowledge, he eventually became an embarrassment to the Republican party.

Republican leadership in 1868 bore little resemblance to the group that had launched the party in the 1850s. The majority of Republicans serving in Congress were former Democrats who knew little about the furor that gave birth to the party. These were politicians who had switched parties mainly because of the war.

The members of the new Republican party wanted to put the war behind them. Their new focus centered on the American dream. They looked to a continent fabulously rich in natural resources. By handing over these resources to wealthy capitalists—made rich from the Civil War—the party stood to become wealthy as well. Included in these resources were mineral rights to mining operations and railroad rights-of-way to the giant railroad interests.

Waste and Greed

As head of the party, Grant was in a position to promote this behavior. Never had a presidential candidate been bought out so completely by campaign contributions from wealthy industrialists. Naively he accepted their money and granted great favors in return. The result was an era of extreme waste in natural resources—lumber, petroleum, forests, gold, silver, iron, and copper. Vast tracts of wilderness, considered to be free goods, were grabbed by those who staked the first claims.

Citizens, fascinated by success and wealth, didn't bother to notice how the wealth was being obtained. Greed by the railroad barons meant nothing when there was such a celebration to take part in over the conquering of the wide open spaces. Although the two parties shared this way of thinking, members of the Republican party were the ones who carried it out. Mark Twain's novel *The Gilded Age* gave this era its appropriate nickname.

As a man who lacked political savvy, Grant sorely needed cabinet members who could fill the void. Instead,

One way the Republican party hoped to enrich itself after the war was by granting rights-of-way to large railroads. Trestles such as this one were needed to create a level passage for railroads over rough terrain.

he gave the positions to personal friends and supporters, which pitted Republican party members against one other. Party leadership was nonexistent.

Although scandal and bribery marked Grant's first term in office, the party renominated him in 1872. His Civil War heroism succeeded in carrying him through the election to serve a second term. His second term, by all accounts was worse than the first.

Scandals

Leading Republican congressmen and officials were exposed in railroad scandals. The secretary of war, William W. Belknap, took part in Indian agency frauds. Still others were indicted in a massive whiskey ring, which resulted in arrests in nearly every state in the Union. Because Grant was bedazzled by millionaires, the party slowly deserted

Mark Twain, in The Gilded Age, *voiced the spirit of the times in these words: "What is the chief end of man?—to get rich. In what way?—dishonestly if we can; honestly if we must."*

the farmers' alliances of the past and turned its attention to Eastern money-holders, who funded the party campaigns.

In 1874 political cartoonist Thomas Nast, drawing a cartoon for *Harper's Weekly,* depicted the Republican party as an elephant. The clever symbol stuck and has been popular and routinely used ever since.

In spite of their many problems, the Republican party led a charmed life until the Panic of 1873. Much of the prosperous economy was built on credit and inflation, creating a shaky foundation. On Black Friday, September 19, the stock market crashed, sending banks and financial institutions into ruin. It took a disaster for the tide to turn. The fiasco brought Democrats together and infused them with new power.

Compromise of 1877

New Democratic strength caused the presidential race of 1876 between Rutherford Hayes of Ohio and Samuel Tilden of New York to be extremely close. Accusations of voting fraud at the polls were made by both parties. The decision regarding the election outcome was, therefore, turned over to the House of Representatives, where commissions investigated irregularities. Procedures dragged on until three days before the inauguration, when Hayes was declared the winner of the election.

As part of the deal-making behind closed doors, the Republicans agreed to withdraw the last of the military forces in the South and to put a Southerner in the cabinet. The Fourteenth and Fifteenth Amendments, which pro-

tected the rights of blacks and which the radical Republicans had fought hard and long to ratify, were ignored. Reconstruction ended. Civil rights would not be enforced in the South again until almost 80 years later. The Democrats were soon referred to as the "solid South," a political group that could wield strong political power.

The elephant first appeared as the symbol of the Republican party in this 1874 cartoon by Thomas Nast. The fox at the bottom represents the Democratic party.

Stalwarts and Half-Breeds

A deep division affected the Republican party in the last decades of the century. The Stalwarts, headed by Roscoe Conkling of New York sought power in government and were strong supporters of the **spoils system.** Half-Breeds, led by James G. Blaine of Maine, made up the other faction. This group pushed for the old Republican ideals.

Fifteen thousand Republicans sought entrance into Chicago's Interstate Industrial Exposition Building, known as the Glass Palace, on June 2, 1880. Because Hayes chose to serve only one term, the position was up for grabs, and the Stalwarts were determined to put Grant back in office. The warring factions became deadlocked in the nomination process, and Grant looked to be the sure winner.

The convention dragged on for nearly six days, when, on the 34th ballot, James A. Garfield was nominated. In a surprise move he was swept into the candidacy. His Stalwart running mate, Chester A. Arthur, was chosen to balance the ticket.

Republicans Retain Power

The heated elections proved that the Democrats were shaking off the shackles of the Civil War and were gaining momentum. Republicans continued to show strength in New England and the Upper Mississippi Valley, where manufacturers and farmers remained loyal voters. A new third party, the Greenback party, claimed over 300,000 votes, demonstrating the awakening of the voice of laborers.

Republicans retained the office of president. In addition, a majority of Republicans ruled the House. In the Senate the Democrats held the majority by one vote. From this time until the election of McKinley, the congressional majority would switch back and forth between the two parties.

James Garfield had little time to prove his leadership abilities; he was assassinated barely three months after his inauguration. The presidency fell to Arthur who, surprisingly, turned out to be an able administrator and an earnest reformer.

The new president succeeded in prosecuting certain post office frauds and was in favor of civil service reform.

Surprising Turnabout

Twice before the century was out, the Democrats returned to the White House for the first time since Buchanan, and both of these nonconsecutive terms (1885–1889 and 1893–1897) were served by Grover Cleveland. In between these terms, Republican Benjamin Harrison, grandson of the ninth president of the United States (William Henry Harrison), was elected president.

When Harrison ran for re-election four years later, Grover Cleveland once again entered the race. During this time, the Populist movement was swelling throughout the nation. In November, many who would have voted Republican threw in with the Populists. The third party garnered over one million popular votes and 22 electoral votes. Democrat Cleveland won the election, becoming the first president to serve a split double term. In yet another historical move, Democrats ruled both houses of Congress for the first time since before the Civil War.

In spite of tough mudslinging party politics during the 1880s and 1890s, the two parties did not differ greatly. Political issues centered around tariffs, free trade, and free coinage of silver—all of which are economic issues. And it was economics that came crashing in on Cleveland just as he began his second term.

Panic of 1893

As had happened 20 years earlier, a black Friday hit the stock market on May 5, 1893. Prices plummeted as traders fought to sell and recoup what they could. The sell-off in stocks and the run on gold (which drained the federal reserve), were much more serious than during the crash of 1873. Cleveland, however, did not act decisively, and his popularity fell as quickly as the stock market prices. By the end of 1893, 600 banks had failed and more than 15,000 businesses had gone bankrupt. Nearly one-fourth of the work force was without jobs.

In the midterm election of 1894, the Republicans swept back into Congress, establishing a solid majority. The adverse circumstances worked in favor of the Republicans and provided them with a new theme. Earlier they had saved the Union; now they would save the nation's economy.

In the mind of many voters, the association between Democrats and hard times would last for three decades. The stage was set for yet another long term of Republican rule.

Although William McKinley won the presidency in 1896 by campaigning from his front porch, the whistle-stop strategy of his opponent, William Jennings Bryan, soon became popular with politicians. Here President McKinley and his party travel to Tuscaloosa, Alabama, c. 1901.

CHAPTER 4

Moving Through Hard Times

THE POLITICAL SUN ONCE again shone brightly on the Republican party as it met for the 1896 convention. The party worked to redefine its position and to commit to severe changes. Having lost twice to Cleveland, it was vital that they regain and hold power.

Party Changes

Although the party still sided with the individual, party leaders had developed ties with special industrial interests. Little by little the party came to represent the views of the rich and powerful. The Republican fight for protective tariffs represented a direct response to big-business interests.

The Democratic party, meanwhile, appealed to Southern farmers, Irish immigrants in the large cities, and urban professionals. In this changing time, the Democrats became the party of working people, the dispossessed, and the common folk.

The Republicans brought forth a trusted candidate in 1896, Governor William McKinley of Ohio. McKinley had been the party's chief **advocate** for the protective tariff for a number of years. Party leaders were united; no negative words were heard. As the convention met in St. Louis, Missouri, McKinley listened to his nomination on his telephone back home in Canton, Ohio. Times truly were changing.

Campaign Strategy

Accompanying McKinley as his faithful campaign manager came millionaire industrialist Marcus Alonzo Hanna. A strong Republican party leader, Hanna lifted the art of campaigning to a new level. Hanna was successful in raising more than $3 million, a record amount for the time. The Hanna propaganda machine turned out 200 different types of pamphlets, targeting them to specific groups and written in different languages. Millions of pieces of campaign literature were distributed. The Republicans outspent their Democratic and Populist opponents. Both the Democrat and Populist parties nominated William Jennings Bryan for president.

McKinley campaigned from his front porch in Canton, where throngs of voters came to hear him speak. Bryan chose a different tack. He created a new campaign strategy by stumping the nation in a railroad whistle-stop campaign.

Hanna's hard work paid off when in November McKinley received the majority of both the popular and the electoral vote. The Grand Old Party (GOP), as it was coming to be called, had won again.

Global Expansion

Foreign policy was not a campaign issue, but it quickly came to the forefront in McKinley's term. A war erupted with Spain over the island of Cuba. Out of this short war emerged a hero named Theodore Roosevelt. Roosevelt organized a volunteer regiment called the Rough Riders, who made front page news for taking San Juan Hill in the midst of heavy fighting. Roosevelt then went on to become governor of New York.

From the victory over Spain, the United States gained Cuba, the Philippines, and Puerto Rico. In another part of the world, the United States annexed the Hawaiian Islands. The boundaries of the country were expanding.

McKinley saw to it that the U.S. Navy was strengthened with new ship building. His sound money policy resulted in the passage of the Gold Standard Act. The economy was once again on the upswing. The president was so popular that when time came for the Republican convention in 1900, the only question was who his running mate would be. Though the Republicans could not know it then, their selection would change history.

Theodore Roosevelt became a national hero when his Rough Riders captured San Juan Hill, Cuba, in 1898.

The Republican Popularity

Teddy Roosevelt did not want to be vice president. He felt he would stagnate in such a position. Furthermore, McKinley didn't want him for a running mate; but the people had other ideas.

When Roosevelt entered the arena of the Great Convention Hall in Philadelphia, the crowd—16,000 strong— broke into an overwhelming roar. Roosevelt took the podium to second the nomination of McKinley for president. McKinley was nominated on the first ballot. Roosevelt was named vice president by acclamation. The team of McKinley and Roosevelt was voted into office by the largest popular majority ever, carrying with them scores of Republican winners in state and local elections.

The entire nation was thrown into shock when on September 6, 1901, their beloved president was shot by an assassin during a reception at the Pan-American Exposition in Buffalo. The noisy, energetic Teddy Roosevelt was now the president and the leader of the Republican party.

A Rough Rider in the White House

At first, party leaders didn't know what to make of this young, boisterous new president. A free thinker, Roosevelt broke with McKinley's domestic policies and supported progressive reforms known as the Square Deal. Appalled at the waste of natural resources, he introduced fresh new ideas about conservation. With the help of a cooperative Congress, he enacted a Pure Food and Drug Act and a Meat Inspection Act. Breaking up the giant industrial monopolies, he gained the label of trust buster.

The Meat Inspection Act was one of Roosevelt's progressive reforms under the Square Deal. Here, pork carcasses in a large Chicago packinghouse have been lined up for inspection.

The people had loved McKinley, but they adored
Teddy Roosevelt. His dynamic energy and enthusiasm in-
fected the entire nation. His election in his own right in
1904 was a foregone conclusion. Party members knew they
had a successful candidate in Roosevelt.

In spite of the fact that Roosevelt acted like a free
thinker, he consistently worked within the confines of the
Republican party. Some people, such as Mark Hanna, in-
tensely disliked the President; others, however, admired
him and worked easily with him.

Passing the Torch

Roosevelt decided not to run for a third term. Instead
he groomed William Howard Taft to take his place and then
left on an African big-game safari. Taft came into office
on Roosevelt's coattails, thanks to the latter's powerful per-
sonality. Taft, however, was unable to work as successfully
with the various factions within the party as had his prede-
cessor. Bickering and backbiting flourished.

When Roosevelt returned to the United States, his dis-
appointment at Taft's inept leadership spurred him to run
against Taft in the Republican primaries of 1908. Party
leaders who held sway over Taft stopped Roosevelt's efforts cold. In his usual impetuous manner, Roosevelt bolted
the party and ran on the Progressive ticket. His new party
acquired the nickname the Bull Moose party.

Because of Roosevelt's magnetic popularity, he succeeded in pulling millions of votes away from the Republican party. As a result Republicans lost control of Congress, and Democrat Woodrow Wilson was elected
president. The blow to the party was devastating.

By the time Wilson ran for re-election, the Republicans had wisely reunited. Wilson, however, won the election again in a close race against Supreme Court Justice
Charles Evans Hughes from New York.

Roosevelt, still an active voice in politics, called out
for the United States's entry into World War I, whereas

William Howard Taft was unable to maintain harmony within the Republican party during his presidency. This portrait shows Taft in later years as Supreme Court chief justice. (He was the only president to hold both offices.)

Wilson held back. When the United States finally did send troops into Europe, Roosevelt lost a son in the fighting. Theodore Roosevelt died on January 6, 1919, just a year after the war was over. His death marked the end of an adventurous era for the Grand Old Party.

Wall Street, New York, on the morning of the stock market crash, October 24, 1929. Republicans, who were blamed for the crash, suffered in the next elections.

5

Republicans Take a Tumble

THE YEAR BEFORE ROOSEVELT'S death, the party took steps to establish permanent national party headquarters in Washington, D.C. Here a staff of publicists and professional fund raisers worked to strengthen the party. After Congress voted to give women the right to vote, a women's division was formed. Later, branches of the club called the Young Republicans were set up.

Republicans Return To Power

The hard work paid off. Senator Warren Harding of Ohio and his running mate, Governor Calvin Coolidge of Connecticut, swept into office with a massive victory in 1920. The Republicans even succeeded in breaking the Solid South by carrying Tennessee.

Over in the Democratic camp, a young man named Franklin Delano Roosevelt, cousin to Teddy, received the nomination for vice president. His name was entered mainly to appeal to Progressives because of his association with Teddy.

The Democrats' loss was due, in part, to Americans' resentment of the restrictions and rationing during the war. They were weary of social experiments and desperately wanted the country to return to normal.

Normalcy

"Normalcy" was a word used often by President Harding. However, beneath the surface of good times and a growing economy lurked widespread corruption. Harding died of food poisoning in 1923, leaving quiet, soft-spoken Coolidge to take over the reins.

Cultural Changes

Rapid social changes during the 1920s rocked the nation. The introduction of automobiles, radios, and movies worked to erode the traditional structures of family, church, and community. Many writers and artists of the time openly scoffed at middle-class values.

Prohibition, to a degree, succeeded in reducing the sale and use of alcohol. Yet it also turned millions of otherwise law-abiding Americans into lawbreakers because many were purchasing or selling illegal moonshine. Prohibition also worked to support and encourage organized crime.

Yet another facet of the 1920s was the get-rich-quick mentality, which was a departure from the conservative, prudent manner of the previous generation. Thousands of Americans rode on the stock market high and thousands of lowly wage earners even owned a few shares.

The growing wealth did not, however, spread to the Midwest. The agricultural depression that followed the war dragged on and deeply split the party. Farmers felt abandoned by their own Republican party members.

The Bottom Falls Out

"Silent Cal," as Calvin Coolidge was known, was easily nominated in 1924. His second term was replete with high protectionist tariffs, lower federal taxes, and major capital building projects. He coined the phrase, "The business of America is business." Meanwhile, he vetoed veterans' and farm bills as being too expensive.

Coolidge surprised the nation by refusing to run for reelection. The lot fell to Herbert Hoover, one of the wealthiest men to ever run for office. Hoover ran on the promise that there would be "a decrease in poverty until we are within hope that it will be abolished from America."

Ironically, the year after he took office, the stock market crash of 1929 occurred, plummeting the nation into a disastrous depression. Hoover believed that aid to the hungry and the unemployed should come from state and local governments and that the federal government should not intervene. Instead, his policy was to lend money to insurance companies, banks, and farm organizations, as well as state, county, and city governments, to stimulate the economy. These policies were highly criticized.

Because the American people came to doubt Hoover's constant assertions that the worst was almost over, their confidence in him ended. The moment the Democrats were waiting for had finally arrived.

The Rise of FDR

Just as the Democrats had been blamed for the Civil War and the Panic of 1873, the Republicans were now blamed for the Stock Market Crash of 1929. Midterm elections saw the Democrats take over the majority in the House and reduce the Republican Senate majority to one.

When the Republicans met for the national convention in Chicago in the summer of 1932, the depression was full-blown. The convention was more like a funeral than the

The depression's effect on Middle America is evident in this 1930s scene from Allen County, Kansas.

usual noisy celebration. Hoover, a strong party leader, ruled with a firm hand, preventing others from contending for the nomination. Newsreel cameras rolled and radio microphones carried the proceedings to the nation as Hoover received the nomination for a second term. As the depression deepened, Hoover returned to Washington to tend to presidential duties, refusing to campaign for office.

A week later, Franklin Delano Roosevelt's acceptance speech for the Democratic nomination for president was broadcast over national radio. When millions of Americans heard his confident, comforting voice, it was as though a storm had passed. Roosevelt touched the heart strings of a grieving nation. In November he won by a landslide and the Democrats became America's majority party.

Through the Depression and the War

Franklin Delano Roosevelt (FDR) quickly set about implementing national programs to turn the tide of the depression. Large government entities, such as the National

Recovery Administration, were created. This organization worked closely with major corporations to revive the economy. Even the powers of the presidential office were expanded. Roosevelt called his program the New Deal.

Politicians who disagreed with the expansion of big government (who were called conservatives) feared this growth. However, the seriousness of the nation's economic condition prevented conservatives from openly opposing the president's emergency measures. The man on the street hailed FDR as the hero of the hour.

Four years later, FDR returned to office receiving the largest margin in a presidential election ever. During FDR's second term, a group of conservatives in Congress worked hard to stop the president's **liberal** bills from passing—specifically, bills that increased the government's powers or increased government spending. This informal group, known as the Conservative Coalition, consisted of both Republicans and Democrats. These conservatives planted the seeds for political changes yet to come.

As the 1940 elections approached, rumblings of war sounded in Europe. FDR, now one of the most popular presidents ever, ran for an unprecedented third term and was voted back into office.

When war broke out in 1941, party differences were forgotten. Citizens and politicians united, rising above politics to win World War II. So united were they, that in 1944 they elected Roosevelt for a historic fourth term.

Less than a month before the end of the war, on April 12, 1945, Franklin Delano Roosevelt died of a stroke. His vice president, Harry S. Truman from Missouri, took the oath of office. Political change was again in the air.

Mushroom cloud over Nagasaki, Japan, after President Truman authorized the dropping of the world's second atomic bomb there in 1945. Truman's hard-line policy in the Cold War era that followed was not favored by all Democrats.

CHAPTER **6**

The Cold War and Beyond

PRESIDENT HARRY TRUMAN BECAME known as the president who used the atomic bombs to end World War II, thus ushering in the atomic age. On its heels came the Cold War, an arms race between the United States and the communist-controlled Soviet Union. Truman's policy leaned toward a hard-line, get-tough stance. Others in his own party strongly disagreed, feeling that peaceful negotiations would accomplish more than military threats would.

"I Like Ike"

Republicans moved in to take advantage of the party split, presenting as their 1952 candidate the beloved war hero, General Dwight D. Eisenhower. The move was similar to the nomination of Grant following the Civil War. Every person in the nation knew and many revered the name of Eisenhower.

Eisenhower-Nixon buttons from the 1952 presidential campaign.

Up through the party ranks came the young vice presidential candidate Richard M. Nixon. Most party members considered him the a middle-of-the-road choice, appealing to both the moderates and the conservatives in the party.

Both Eisenhower and Nixon traveled thousands of miles in their campaign efforts. Television cameras now carried the action to the public, and a clever campaign ad used the slogan, "I like Ike." The Eisenhower-Nixon team worked its magic in November, gaining a strong majority vote and bringing Republican control to Congress as well.

Though grateful to be back in the White House, many party leaders were unhappy with the leadership. Because the former general had a distaste for politics, Eisenhower did little to build up the party. Conservatives saw Eisenhower's policies as akin to the liberal leanings of FDR. This party division continued to deepen. Conservatives wanted government spending cut back; Eisenhower chose simply to hold the line on spending.

In spite of Eisenhower's re-election in 1956, the Republicans lost control of both houses of Congress. For the next 40 years, the Democrats would control Congress.

Eisenhower in 1956 campaigning for his second term as president. Many Republicans were dissatisfied with the way he led the party.

Turbulent Times

In the election of 1960, voter count was so close between Democrat John F. Kennedy and his opponent, Republican Richard Nixon, that a recount was seriously considered. Kennedy came into office with a margin of 113,000 votes out of almost seventy million cast. Once again, the Republicans were shut out.

The 1960s were fraught with national problems. Protests over involvement in the Vietnam War and struggles for civil rights for blacks resulted in riots and bloodshed. Three politically fueled assassinations occurred during this decade, that of President Kennedy, civil rights leader Martin Luther King Jr., and the Democratic presidential candidate of 1968, Robert Kennedy.

Republican Split Deepens

The turbulence of the times was reflected in the inner turmoil of the Republican party. Conservative Barry Goldwater of Arizona was determined to take the party away from the Easterners and move the party back to the common people. After Goldwater won the nomination in 1964, disgruntled Republican moderates, led by New York Governor Nelson Rockefeller, offered very little support to their candidate. As a result Goldwater was badly defeated by Lyndon B. Johnson.

In 1968 the party's answer to heal the deep split was to nominate that middle-of-the-road man, Richard Nixon. He ran against Hubert Humphrey of California and Governor George Wallace of Alabama. As a protest against the civil rights movement, Wallace formed a third-party group and received 10 million votes. Nixon won the election by a small majority, then faced a Democratic Congress. He became the first new president since 1848 to take office with both houses controlled by the opposing party.

Disgrace

Nixon dealt the party an almost fatal blow when he became the first president ever to resign from office. Barely two years after his re-election in 1972, in the heat of the Watergate scandal, Nixon announced his resignation. The presidency went to Vice President Gerald Ford. Ford had only recently become vice president because of the scandal that resulted in Spiro Agnew's being removed from office.

Ford faced challenges that had no quick, easy answers. History would show that in spite of much criticism and party opposition, Ford handled the office well. His full and open pardon of Nixon on September 8, 1974, probably did more damage to Ford than had any other of his actions while he was in office. The public was still too hurt and angry to accept the pardon.

The Republican party was at a low ebb. Some predicted that it was headed toward total ruin.

A Common President

A peanut farmer from Georgia, professing to be a born-again Christian, became the Democrats' answer in 1976.

Although James (Jimmy) Carter had served as a senator and governor, he was first and foremost a businessman. He ran on the promise of bringing decency and order back to the White House—a refreshing note following the scandals of the Nixon administration.

Vietnam War protesters in Washington, D.C., 1971.

Problems arose almost immediately for Carter. He did little to build party unity and was aloof from his fellow Democrats in Congress. His administration inherited problems of economic recession, but his policies did nothing to support the sagging economy. Complications increased when a number of American hostages were taken captive in Iran. The public lost confidence in Carter as a strong leader partially because of the hostage crisis.

Evangelicals came together during this time under the leadership of religious leader Jerry Falwell. Calling themselves the Moral Majority, they worked at the grassroots level to bring morality back to the nation's political scene. They succeeded in registering millions of voters—four million in 1980 alone. As a central organization, the Moral Majority folded in 1989.

Strengthening the Foundation

During the 1970s and 1980s, because of several changes, support for the political parties fell drastically. Television became the source for political information. Neighborhood political wards and precincts, which were prevalent in the 1930s and 1940s, disappeared. The power of special-interest groups increased within the two parties. Both the Democrats and Republicans expanded their central offices and increased their staffs. This highly centralized organization did not rely as much on the grassroots movements, thus individual members felt no close affiliation with their parties.

Following the Watergate scandal, Congress passed a campaign finance act, which limited the amount of money an individual could give to a candidate or a party. No longer could a party look to a few wealthy persons for support, as they had in the past.

These were the challenges that met William Brock of Tennessee when he took over as Republican National Chairman in 1977. Brock instituted a direct-mail campaign to party supporters. The program was a huge success, bringing in millions of dollars of needed contributions. These funds were then used to expand party outreach with monthly and quarterly publications. In addition Brock paid special attention to state and local campaigns and stepped in to assist candidates when needed. Although party support was not nearly as strong as it had been in decades past, it had at least stopped shrinking.

Reagan's Success

Those who had pronounced the Republican party finished had not counted on the downfall of Jimmy Carter. By election time 1980, even the Democrats were discouraged. From out of the wings, as though on cue, came former Hollywood movie star and California governor Ronald Reagan. Reagan's conservative voice had been heard in

Ronald Reagan in his earlier career as a Hollywood actor. His overwhelming victory in the 1980 election gave a great boost to conservative Republicans.

support of Goldwater years earlier. Most Americans were more than ready for the change.

Once Reagan announced his candidacy, he swept through the primaries winning victory after victory. He easily won the presidential nomination and named George Bush of Texas as his running mate. Earning the nickname of the Great Communicator, Reagan won the hearts of millions who heard him speak.

Reagan inherited the support of groups who had been for Goldwater in 1964. In addition two new groups came flocking to his side: Catholics and other pro-life people, who were disturbed over the Supreme Court ruling that legalized abortion, and evangelical Protestants, who were concerned that American culture was turning away from the faith of the Founding Fathers.

Reagan's victory in November was so great that Carter conceded the contest even before the West Coast finished voting. At last the conservative Republicans had a taste of victory.

Party Man

To the benefit of the Republican party, Reagan had always been a strong party man (after having switched parties in 1962). As governor of California, he worked to build up the state party by campaigning for moderate and conservative candidates alike. After his nomination for president, he continued to include Republicans running for congressional and state offices in his campaign. This attention was rewarded with united support from both the House and Senate, with even more help from a few conservative Democrats.

Reagan easily won re-election in 1984. One of the largest new groups to cast its votes for a Republican candidate that fall were those under the age of thirty. Young voters, who usually voted Democratic, crossed over to support Reagan. These switches in party voting, as time would tell, were not permanent. Party loyalty looked to be a thing of the past.

Losing Ground

The Republicans nominated Vice President George Bush as their candidate for president in 1988. His running mate was a young senator from Indiana, Dan Quayle. An interesting addition to those running in the Republican primaries was evangelist Pat Robertson who supported an anti-abortion and school prayer platform. Although Robertson failed to receive the nomination, he went on to form an organization called the Christian Coalition. Much like Falwell's Moral Majority group, the Christian Coalition provided a mouthpiece for conservatives concerned about the moral decline of the nation.

Bush succeeded in defeating his opponent, Walter Mondale of Minnesota, but seats were lost in both the House and the Senate, marking the close of the popular Reagan era.

Bush prepared for the last battle of the Cold War by launching the Gulf War against Saddam Hussein of Iraq. The military buildup of the Reagan years and the foreign diplomacy of President Bush paid off. Saving the small nation of Kuwait from the aggressive Iraqi attack created new popularity for Bush.

The domestic scene, however, presented a different picture. Bush raised taxes after publicly pledging not to do so, turning even his own party members against him. This move made it difficult for him to win their confidence at the 1992 national convention. Retaining Quayle on the ticket, Bush was renominated. To his dismay Bush found himself in a race with not only a young Democrat from Arkansas, Bill Clinton, but a third-party candidate from Texas, billionaire Ross Perot.

Although Clinton was not widely known and was encumbered by a number of negatives against him, the entry of Perot into the race worked in Clinton's favor. Perot came into the race under the banner of the Reform party, endorsing much of the Republican platform. Disgruntled voters, hungry for a new choice, voted for Perot. Perot received about 19 million votes, which threw the race to the Democrats. The Democrats also took over the majority in both houses of Congress. The scene was similar to Teddy Roosevelt's third-party attempt, which gave the presidency to Wilson.

Democrat Bill Clinton (left), third-party candidate Ross Perot (center), and Republican President George Bush end their final debate in the 1992 presidential race on a lighter note.

As before, when the odds were against them, the Republicans redoubled their efforts at the grassroots level. Mounting an aggressive midterm election campaign in 1994, they reseized control of the House and Senate. Two years later, however, Senator Robert Dole of Kansas was unable to unseat Clinton in the presidential election.

Once again the tide had turned against the Republicans. If history is any indicator, however, the party will regroup, work hard, and revive to make yet another strong showing in the years ahead.

Recap

Since the party's inception in 1856, Republicans have occupied the White House for 80 years. The Grand Old Party has been the smaller, but the more unified, of the two major parties. The Democratic party is made up of many smaller special-interest groups, making it more fragmented. In the beginning the strength of the Republican party came from New England and the Midwest. After World War II, support grew in the South and West.

Often called the party of Lincoln, the Republican party has historically been the more conservative group, generally in favor of free enterprise and against the welfare state. Most Republicans believe that less government is better government and that they should intervene only if individuals are incapable of helping themselves.

Although U.S. political parties are a long way from being perfect, they serve as a means of conveying the messages of political leaders and giving voters choices and voices at the polls. Through the years the Republicans have had their share of strong leaders and weak leaders, successful legislation and unsuccessful legislation, and good times and bad times. In spite of it all, the Republican party has and will continue to play a vital role in the political system of this great democracy.

Glossary

Abolitionist—A person who believes the practice of slavery should be ended.

Advocate—To speak in favor of a person or policy.

Campaign—An organized activity to gain a political goal or office.

Candidate—A person who seeks or is nominated for an office.

Coalition—A combination or fusion into one body.

Compromise—A settlement of differences in which each side gives up some claims and accepts some demands of the other.

Conservative—A political group that favors more traditional values.

Faction—An organization or group within a larger group that often seeks its own ends.

Liberal—A political party that advocates more broad-minded social views.

Nominate—To choose a person as a candidate for an election or an office.

Party platform—A formal declaration of principles by a political party or a candidate.

Proviso—A clause in a document making a qualification, condition, or restriction.

Sovereignty—Complete independence and self-government.

Spoils system—Rewarding political supporters with jobs or appointments.

Tariff—A system of duties imposed by the government on imported or exported goods.

Further Reading

Blue, Rose, and Corinne Naden. *Who's That in the White House? The Modern Years: 1969 to 2001.* Austin, TX: Raintree Steck-Vaughn, 1998.

Heath, David. *Elections in the United States.* Mankato, MN: Capstone Press, 1999.

Henry, Christopher E. *Presidential Conventions.* New York: Franklin Watts, 1996.

Jones, Veda Boyd. *Government and Politics.* Philadelphia: Chelsea House, 1999.

Kronenwetter, Michael. *Political Parties of the United States.* Springfield, NJ: Enslow Publishers, 1996.

Lindop, Edward. *Political Parties.* New York: Twenty-First Century Books, 1996.

Steins, Richard. *Our Elections.* Brookfield, CT: Millbrook Press, 1994.

Index

ABOUT THE AUTHOR: Norma Jean Lutz, who lives in Tulsa, Oklahoma, has been writing professionally since 1977. She is the author of more than 250 short stories and articles as well as 36 fiction and nonfiction books. Of all the writing she does, she most enjoys writing children's books.

SENIOR CONSULTING EDITOR Arthur M. Schlesinger, jr. is the leading American historian of our time. He won the Pulitzer Prize for his book *The Age of Jackson* (1945) and again for *A Thousand Days* (1965). This chronicle of the Kennedy Administration also won a National Book Award. Professor Schlesinger is the Albert Schweitzer Professor of the Humanities at the City University of New York, and has been involved in several other Chelsea House projects, including the REVOLUTIONARY WAR LEADERS and COLONIAL LEADERS series.

Picture Credits